Sweet as (Maple) Syrup

Syrup

40 Sweet Recipes

BY: Nancy Silverman

COPYRIGHT NOTICES

||||||||||||||||||||||||||||||||||||||||||||||||||||||||||||||||||||

My Heartfelt Thanks and A Special Reward for Your Purchase!

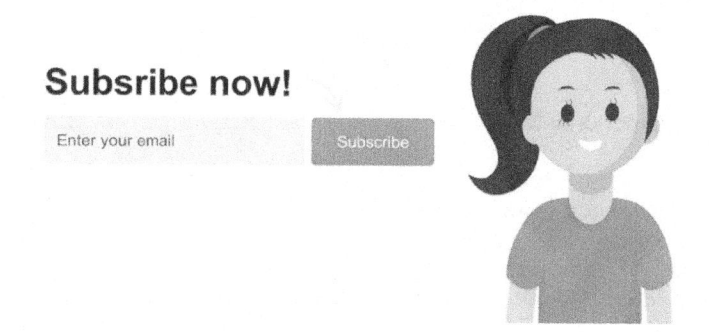

https://nancy.gr8.com

My heartfelt thanks at purchasing my book and I hope you enjoy it! As a special bonus, you will now be eligible to receive books absolutely free on a weekly basis! Get started by entering your email address in the box above to subscribe. A notification will be emailed to you of my free promotions, no purchase necessary! With little effort, you will be eligible for free and discounted books daily. In addition to this amazing gift, a reminder will be sent 1-2 days before the offer expires to remind you not to miss out. Enter now to start enjoying this special offer!

Table of Contents

Chapter I - Syrups and Sauces

||||||||||||||||||||||||||||||||||||||||||||||||||||||||||||||||||||||||

(1) Maple Syrup Yogurt Sauce

This sauce is very versatile; you can spoon it onto oatmeal, pancakes, or waffles. It also tastes great on its own with a fruit garnish.

Serving Size: 1 cup

Preparation Time: 3mins

Ingredient List:

- ⅔ cup Greek yogurt
- 2½ teaspoons maple syrup
- ¼ teaspoons vanilla extract
- ¼ teaspoons cinnamon

||||||||||||||||||||||||||||||||||||||||||||||||||||||||||||||||

Instructions:

1. In a large sized mixing bowl, whisk the yogurt with the maple syrup, vanilla extract, and cinnamon until silky smooth and fully incorporated.

2. Store in the fridge in an airtight, re-sealable container for up to 7 days.

(2) Blueberry Maple Syrup Sauce

A berry infused maple syrup sauce to jazz up waffles and pancakes.

Serving Size: 2-4 cups

Preparation Time: 35mins

Ingredient List:

- 5 cup blueberries (de-stemmed, washed, divided)
- 1 cup cold water
- 1 cup granulated sugar
- 2 teaspoons lemon juice
- 2 teaspoons pure maple syrup

||||||||||||||||||||||||||||||||||||||||||||||||||||||||||||||||||||

Instructions:

1. Put 4 cups of blueberries along with 1 cup of cold water in a large pan over moderate to high heat.

2. Using a potato masher, mash the berries to release their juices.

3. Bring the blueberries to boil, and reduce heat to moderate-low. Simmer the blueberries for 15 minutes, while occasionally stirring. You will notice that they will become a darker color.

4. Using a ladle remove the blueberries from the pot and using a mesh strainer, strain to remove their skins.

5. Return the berry liquid to the pan and add the sugar along with the lemon juice, and maple syrup. Bring to simmer, occasionally stirring, until the syrup thickens to your preferred consistency.

6. Remove the pan from the heat; add the remaining cup of berries, gently stirring to incorporate.

7. The sauce can be served either warm or slightly chilled.

(3) Whiskey Maple Cream Sauce

Whip us this cheeky whiskey sauce to serve over waffles or pies.

Serving Size: 12

Preparation Time: 55mins

Ingredient List:

- 1 ½ cups heavy cream
- 5 tablespoons pure maple syrup
- 3 tablespoons light corn syrup
- 1 tablespoon whiskey

||||||||||||||||||||||||||||||||||||||||||||||||||||||||||||||||||||

Instructions:

1. In a medium-sized pan combine the heavy cream along with the maple syrup and corn syrup, stirring to incorporate.

2. Cook the mixture over moderate to low heat, continually stirring for 15 minutes, or until the sauce bubbles thickens and reduces.

3. Once the sauce has thickened, take the pan off the heat and add the whiskey, stirring to combine. Return the pan to the heat and stir for 2-3 minutes.

4. Pour the sauce into a suitable container, allow to cool and transfer to the refrigerator until chilled.

5. Stir well before serving.

(4) Maple-Bacon Praline Syrup

Drizzle this syrup on to scrambled eggs and pancakes to turn a boring brunch into a masterpiece.

Serving Size: 2

Preparation Time: 6mins

Ingredient List:

- ½ cup butter
- ½ cup chopped pecans
- ½ cup pure maple syrup
- 2 thick hickory-smoked bacon slices (cooked, crumbled)

||||||||||||||||||||||||||||||||||||||||||||||||||||||||||||||||||||||||||

Instructions:

1. In a saucepan over moderate to low heat, while stirring, cook the butter along with the pecans, maple syrup, and bacon for 5 minutes; until the sugar has melted and the sauce is incorporated.

2. Serve.

(5) Salted Maple Caramel Sauce

A buttery sweet, yet salty caramel sauce. Serve over lots of different types of breakfast pancakes and desserts.

Serving Size: ½-⅔ cup

Preparation Time: 20mins

Ingredients

- 2 cups grade b maple syrup
- ¼ cup unsalted butter
- ½ cup heavy cream
- 2 large pinches sea salt

||||||||||||||||||||||||||||||||||||||||||||||||||||||||||||||||||||

Instructions:

1. Add the maple syrup to a large, heavy bottom, deep-sided pan and bring to boil over moderate heat. Allow to softly boil for 15 minutes. Stir every couple of minutes with a heatproof kitchen utensil; this will reduce the bubbles. The mixture will look very much like candy at the softball stage.

2. Add the butter and stir until melted. Next, add the cream, continually stirring.

3. Add the salt and stir to combine.

4. Serve.

(6) Maple Date Caramel Sauce

Pile or drizzle this rich sauce over cookies, ice cream, brownies or your morning oats

Serving Size: 2/3 cup

Preparation Time: 10mins

Ingredient List:

- 10 soft, fresh medjool dates (pitted)
- 3 tablespoons pure maple syrup
- 1 tablespoon unsalted butter (melted)
- ¼ teaspoons salt

||||||||||||||||||||||||||||||||||||||||||||||||||||||||||||||||||||

Instructions:

1. Add the medjool dates along with the maple syrup, melted butter and salt to a food processor and process until silky, for between 7-10 minutes, scraping down the sides of the bowl/jug as needed.

2. Transfer the sauce to a re-sealable, airtight glass container.

3. Store in the refrigerator for up to 14 days and use as needed (soften if necessary by gently heating in the microwave).

(7) Peanut Butter Maple Syrup

You won't be able to resist this pot to pancake sauce.

Serving Size: 6

Preparation Time: 15mins

Ingredient List:

- 6 tablespoons unsalted butter
- ¼ cup whole milk
- ¼ cup heavy cream
- ¼ cup organic maple syrup
- 2 teaspoons vanilla
- ¾ cup sugar
- ½ cup smooth peanut butter

||||||||||||||||||||||||||||||||||||||||||||||||||||||||||||||||||

Instructions:

1. In a large sized saucepan over moderate heat, add the first 6 ingredients (butter through sugar) and stir until incorporated.

2. Add the peanut butter and bring to a boil.

3. Reduce the heat, and simmer for 60 seconds.

4. Serve over pancakes.

(8) Maple Praline Pecan Sauce

A new England recipe that will transform a plain breakfast into a showstopper. Delicious served over pancakes and waffles.

Serving Size: 1¼ cups

Preparation Time: 15mins

Ingredient List:

- ¾ cup pure maple syrup
- 1 cup heavy whipping cream
- ½ cup pecans (chopped)
- 1 teaspoon vanilla bean paste

|||||||||||||||||||||||||||||||||||||||||||||||||||||||||||||||||

Instructions:

1. In a medium saucepan combine the maple syrup along with the whipping cream and bring to boil over moderate heat.

2. Boil rapidly, occasionally stirring for 15 minutes.

3. Allow to cool.

4. Add the chopped pecans and vanilla bean paste and stir until combined.

5. Serve the sauce warm.

(9) Maple Syrup Cranberry Sauce

Think outside the box about how to serve this sauce. It's not just for savory dishes; it's good on yogurt and pancakes, too.

Serving Size: 6

Preparation Time: 25mins

Ingredient List:

- 1 cup water
- 1 cup maple syrup
- 1 (12 ounce) bag fresh cranberries
- 1 tablespoon brown sugar
- 1 dash lemon juice
- 1 tablespoon brandy

||||||||||||||||||||||||||||||||||||||||||||||||||||||||||||||||||

Instructions:

1. In a medium-sized saucepan combine the water along with the maple syrup and bring to boil.

2. Add the cranberries to the pan and cook the mixture at a boil, for between 10-15 minutes, or until the berries begin to pop.

3. Add the brown sugar, while stirring, together with the lemon juice and cranberries. Continue stirring until the sugar has dissolved.

4. Serve.

(10) Maple Syrup and Banana Sauce

Use this warm fruity sauce as topping for yogurt, cake or even ice-cream.

Serving Size: 12

Preparation Time: 10mins

Ingredient List:

- ¼ cup butter
- ¼ cup brown sugar
- ½ cup maple syrup
- 2 dashes ground cinnamon
- 3 ripe bananas (peeled, sliced)

||||||||||||||||||||||||||||||||||||||||||||||||||||||||||||||||||||||

Instructions:

1. In a large pan or skillet over moderate heat, melt the butter.

2. Stir in the sugar along with the syrup, and cinnamon into the melted butter, for 3-4 minutes until the sugar has dissolved.

3. Add the banana and stir well to evenly coat, simmer until hot for a couple of minutes.

4. Serve warm.

Chapter II – Smoothies

||||||||||||||||||||||||||||||||||||||||||||||||||||||||||||||||||||||||||||

(11) Wild Blueberry Minty Maple Smoothie

Go wild with this smoothie; blueberries and maple syrup are a match made in heaven.

Serving Size: 1-2

Preparation Time: 6mins

Ingredient List:

- 1 medium banana (chopped and frozen)
- 1 cup frozen wild blueberries
- ½ cup pure maple water
- ½ cup almond milk
- ¼ teaspoons peppermint essence
- 1 teaspoon maple syrup
- Mint leaves (to garnish)

||||||||||||||||||||||||||||||||||||||||||||||||||||||||||||||||||||||||

Instructions:

1. In a food blender, process all 6 smoothie ingredients until smooth.

2. Pour into a tall glass, garnish with mint and enjoy.

(12) Blueberry Lavender Smoothie

A protein smoothie is a perfect way to start the day especially when it includes superfoods such as spinach and blueberries with maple syrup adding sweetness.

Serving Size: 2

Preparation Time:

Ingredient List:

- 1 cup unsweetened almond milk
- 1 teaspoon dried culinary lavender
- ⅓ cup vanilla protein powder
- 1 cup blueberries
- 1 cup spinach
- 1 tablespoon pure maple syrup
- 1 cup ice

||||||||||||||||||||||||||||||||||||||||||||||||||||||||||||||||||||||||||

Instructions:

1. Place all 7 ingredients in a blender, in recipe list order and process until silky smooth.

(13) Sweet Potato Smoothie

A sweet potato smoothie, to drink any time of the day or night; at breakfast, as a snack or for dessert.

Serving Size: 1

Preparation Time: 4mins

Ingredient List:

- 1 ripe banana (peeled)
- 1 cup roasted sweet potato puree
- 1 tablespoon maple syrup
- 1 cup unsweetened milk of choice
- ½ teaspoons vanilla extract
- Dash cinnamon
- Ice cubes

||||||||||||||||||||||||||||||||||||||||||||||||||||||||||||||||||||||

Instructions:

1. All ingredients in recipe list order to a blender and process until smooth.

2. Pour into a glass and enjoy.

(14) Cinnamon Bun Smoothie

Wow, this breakfast beverage takes exactly like a cinnamon bun but with fewer calories.

Serving Size: 2

Preparation Time: 2mins

Ingredient List:

- 2 frozen bananas (peeled, each cut into 4 pieces)
- 2 cups unsweetened almond milk
- 1 teaspoon ground cinnamon
- ½ teaspoons vanilla extract
- ½ teaspoons pure maple syrup
- Cinnamon sticks (to garnish)

||||||||||||||||||||||||||||||||||||||||||||||||||||||||||||||||||||||||

Instructions:

1. Combine all 5 smoothie ingredients in a blender. Blend until silky smooth, adding additional almond milk if needed.

2. Pour the smoothie into 2 tall glasses, garnish with a cinnamon stick and enjoy.

(15) Strawberry Shortcake Overnight Oatmeal Smoothie

All the flavor of a yummy strawberry shortcake in a deliciously sweet slurpable smoothie.

Serving Size: 1

Preparation Time: 8hours 5mins

Ingredient List:

- ¾ cup unsweetened vanilla almond milk
- ⅓ cup rolled oats
- ½ tablespoons natural almond butter
- ½ - 1 tablespoon maple syrup
- ½ teaspoons vanilla extract
- Pinch of salt
- 1 cup frozen strawberries
- Chopped nuts (optional)

Instructions:

1. Prepare the smoothie the night before, by adding the first 6 ingredients to a bowl (almond milk through salt). Stir to combine and cover. Transfer the bowl to the refrigerator overnight.

2. The following day, remove the bowl from the fridge and place in a food blender.

3. Add the frozen strawberries to the blender and blitz on high speed until creamy smooth. Adding a splash more milk if needed.

4. Pour the smoothie into a glass and add toppings of choice.

(16) Frozen Hot Chocolate Banana Bowl

Smoothie bowls are the latest trend. You can add your favorite toppings including fruit and nuts.

Serving Size: 1

Preparation Time: 8hours 5mins

Ingredient List:

- ¾ cup unsweetened vanilla almond milk
- ⅓ cup rolled oats
- 2 tablespoons unsweetened cocoa powder
- 1 tablespoon chia seeds
- ½-1 tablespoon maple syrup
- ½ teaspoons vanilla extract
- 1 medium ripe banana (frozen)
- 2 ice cubes
- Chopped nuts (to serve, optional)

||||||||||||||||||||||||||||||||||||||||||||||||||||||||||||||||||||||

Instructions:

1. Add the first 6 ingredients (milk through vanilla extract) to your food blender and blitz to combine. Transfer to a bowl and refrigerate overnight.

2. When you are ready to enjoy, return the smoothie to the blender and add the frozen banana along with the ice cubes and blitz until the oats have broken down and are silky.

3. Add a splash more almond milk if you feel the smoothie is a little thick.

4. Serve scattered with your favorite toppings.

(17) Spinach, Avocado, And Maple Smoothie Bowl

A super green smoothie sweetened with maple syrup is pretty delicious.

Serving Size: 1

Preparation Time: 4mins

Ingredient List:

- 1 large handful fresh spinach leaves (washed)
- 1 large ripe pear (sliced, frozen)
- ½ large avocado (peeled, pitted, chopped)
- ⅓-½ cup half fat yogurt
- 1 tablespoon pure maple syrup
- ½ cup filtered water (chilled)

IIIIIIIIIIIIIIIIIIIIIIIIIIIIIIIIIIIIIIIIIIIIIIIIIIIIIIIIIIIIIIIII

Instructions:

1. Add the spinach, pear, avocado, yogurt, maple syrup and ¼ cup of filtered water to a blender. Blend until silky; add more water until you achieve your preferred consistency.

2. Serve in a bowl with your favorite toppings.

(18) Key Lime Pie Smoothie

At just under 250 calories per single serving what better way to start the day?

Serving Size: 1

Preparation Time: 3mins

Ingredient List:

- 4 ounces almond milk
- ¼ teaspoons pure vanilla extract
- ½ teaspoons pure maple syrup
- 1 small banana (partially frozen*, peeled)
- ¼ avocado (peeled, pitted, chopped)
- 1 lime (peeled, deseeded)

||||||||||||||||||||||||||||||||||||||||||||||||||||||||||||||||||

Instructions:

1. First, add the almond milk, vanilla and maple syrup to your food blender, followed by the fruit.

2. Blitz until silky and serve.

* allow the bananas to thaw a little (but not all the way) as this improves the texture of the smoothie.

(19) Maple Walnut Coffee Smoothie

A big old caffeine kick from this thick and tasty vegan smoothie.

Serving Size: 1

Preparation Time: 6mins

Ingredient List:

- 2 tablespoons walnuts
- 2 tablespoons old-fashioned rolled oats
- ¾ cup plain, unsweetened almond milk
- ½ tablespoons instant powdered coffee
- 1 pinch sea salt
- 1 packet stevia
- 1 teaspoon maple extract
- ½ teaspoons vanilla extract
- 2 medjool dates (pitted, coarsely chopped)
- 6-8 ice cubes

|||||||||||||||||||||||||||||||||||||||||||||||||||||||||||||||||||||||||||

Instructions:

1. Add the walnuts along with the rolled oats to a food blender and process, on pulse until a powder is formed.

2. Add the following 7 ingredients (almond through dates) and blitz until silky.

3. Add the ice and on pulse, process.

4. Transfer the smoothie to a tall glass and enjoy.

(20) Maple Chai Spice Smoothie Bowl

Maple and chai are the perfect pairing, and this maple chai smoothie bowl makes for a really satisfying breakfast.

Serving Size: 1

Preparation Time: 8mins

Ingredient List:

Smoothie bowl:

- 1 large ripe banana (chopped, frozen)
- 1 tablespoon pure maple syrup
- 1 tablespoon chia seeds
- 2 teaspoons almond butter
- ½ teaspoons chai spice*
- 1 cup almond milk (unsweetened)
- Small handful ice cubes

Toppings:

- Granola
- Toasted coconut
- Berries

IIIIIIIIIIIIIIIIIIIIIIIIIIIIIIIIIIIIIIIIIIIIIIIIIIIIIIIIIIIIIIIIIIIIIIIIII

Instructions:

1. Add all smoothie ingredients into a blender and blitz until smooth.

2. Transfer the smoothie to your breakfast bowl and scatter with your chosen toppings.

* for the chai spice blend (1/4 cup): combine 1 tablespoon each of ground cinnamon, allspice, cardamom, ginger and cloves and store in a re-sealable airtight jar.

Chapter III – Breakfast and Brunch

||||||||||||||||||||||||||||||||||||||||||||||||||||||||||||||||||||||||||||

(21) Stuffed French Toast with Peach Bourbon Maple Syrup

French toast goes gourmet with this sweet peach and maple syrup adult breakfast.

Serving Size: 9

Preparation Time: 35mins

Ingredient List:

Syrup:

- 2 medium ripe peaches (peeled, pitted, diced)
- ½ cup pure maple syrup
- 1 tablespoon bourbon

French toast:

- 1 (16 ounce) loaf challah bread (round edges cut off, sliced 1" thick)
- 1 ounce cream cheese (whipped)
- 2 cups whole milk
- 1 large egg (beaten lightly)
- 1 teaspoon cinnamon
- 1 teaspoon vanilla essence

|||||||||||||||||||||||||||||||||||||||||||||||||||||||||||||||||||||

Instructions:

1. To make the syrup: in a small pan over moderate heat, heat the peaches along with the maple syrup and bourbon. Bring to boil, reduce heat to simmer and cook for 5-6 minutes. Put to one side while keeping warm and covered.

2. Carefully slice a pocket into each of the pieces of challah bread, taking care not to cut through. Using clean fingers gently make the opening a little larger and spread 1 tablespoon of whipped cream cheese into each pocket. Set to one side.

3. Over moderate heat, preheat a skillet.

4. Pour the milk into a pie dish and whisk in the lightly beaten eggs along with the cinnamon and vanilla until incorporated.

5. In batches, dip the slices of bread in the milk mixture, turning to evenly coat on each side, shake off any excess.

6. Lightly mist the pan with nonstick cooking spray and lay the bread in the pan, taking care not to overcrowd the pan.

7. Cook each slice for between 2 and 3 minutes each side, or until lightly golden and just crisp.

8. Remove from the pan, place on a wire baking rack set over a baking tray, and in an oven set at 200 degrees f, and keep warm.

9. Repeat the process until every bread slice is cooked.

10. Serve with plenty of warm bourbon syrup.

(22) Apple 'N Maple Breakfast Bread Pudding

This bread pudding is a welcome change from the usual pancakes and breakfast waffles and is the ideal dish to serve to guests over the holidays.

Serving Size: 2

Preparation Time: 55mins

Ingredient List:

- 2 tablespoons butter (divided)
- 2 granny smith apples (peeled, cored, quartered, cut into 1/3" slices)
- ¼ cup cholesterol egg fat-free substitute
- ½ cup 1% low-fat milk
- 2 tablespoons pure maple syrup
- ½ teaspoons vanilla extract
- ¼ teaspoons ground cinnamon
- 2 slices whole grain bread
- Confectioner's sugar (for dusting)

||||||||||||||||||||||||||||||||||||||||||||||||||||||||||||||||||||||||||

Instructions:

1. Preheat the main oven to 350 degrees f. Lightly grease a 1-quart casserole dish with 1 teaspoon of butter.

2. In a large frying pan or skillet, over moderate to high heat, melt 1 more teaspoon of butter. Add the apples, occasionally stirring, for 5 minutes until golden.

3. In the meantime, whisk in the egg substitute together with the milk, maple syrup, vanilla extract, and cinnamon. Set to one side.

4. In a bowl, toss the cooked apples with the bread and pour the egg mixture over the top of the bread, tossing to coat evenly.

5. Place the mixture in the prepared casserole dish, cover and bake in the oven for 35 minutes.

6. Remove the cover, and bake for a further 5 minutes, or until golden brown.

7. Dust with confectioners' sugar and serve.

(23) Pumpkin Breakfast Soufflé

Enjoy a healthy start to your day with this comforting and super delicious soufflé.

Serving Size: 6

Preparation Time: 40mins

Ingredient List:

- Coconut oil (to grease)
- 5 medium eggs
- ¾ cup pumpkin purée
- 1 teaspoon vanilla extract
- 1 teaspoon pumpkin spice
- 3 tablespoons maple syrup

||||||||||||||||||||||||||||||||||||||||||||||||||||||||||||||||||

Instructions:

1. Preheat the main oven to 350 degrees f. Lightly grease a 9" pie pan with coconut oil.

2. Add the eggs, pumpkin puree, vanilla extract, spice and maple syrup to a blender and process until the mixture is silky and an even consistency.

3. Transfer the mixture to the prepared pan and bake in the oven for 30-35 minutes or until the eggs are set, and the top and edges of the soufflé are lightly golden.

4. Set to one side to cool for 4-5 minutes and enjoy warm.

(24) Bacon Breakfast Sandwich with Maple Mustard and Fried Egg

Canadian bacon with tangy maple mustard and a fried egg makes for a satisfying breakfast or brunch sandwich.

Serving Size: 1

Preparation Time: 12mins

Ingredient List:

- 2 rashers Canadian bacon
- 1 medium egg
- 1 tablespoon grainy mustard
- 1 teaspoon maple syrup
- 2 slices bread (lightly toasted)

||||||||||||||||||||||||||||||||||||||||||||||||||||||||||||||||||||||

Instructions:

1. In a frying pan or skillet, fry the bacon and set to one side.

2. Add the egg to the pan and fry to your desired level of doneness.

3. In a small bowl mix the mustard with the syrup until smooth.

4. Arrange the cooked bacon between 2 slices of lightly toasted bread and arrange the fried egg on top along with a dollop of mustard maple mix.

(25) Poppy Seed and Buckwheat Pancakes with Strawberry Salsa and Balsamic Maple Syrup

Buckwheat adds depth of flavor and accompanied by crunch poppy seeds and sweet strawberry salsa these pancakes go far beyond a regular breakfast dish.

Serving Size: 6-8

Preparation Time: 30mins

Ingredient List:

Strawberry salsa:

- 1 cup strawberries (hulled, diced)
- 2 green onions (minced)
- 1 jalapeno (seeded, minced)
- 6 basil leaves, minced
- Juice 1 small lime
- ¼ teaspoons salt

Pancakes (dry ingredients):

- 1 cup buckwheat flour
- 1 cup oat flour
- ¼ teaspoons salt
- 2 teaspoons baking soda
- 3 tablespoons poppy seeds
- Pancakes (wet ingredient):
- 1 cup unsweetened nut milk
- 1 ripe banana
- 1 tablespoon olive oil
- 1 teaspoon vanilla
- 1 medium egg (lightly beaten)
- Butter (for the pan)
- Balsamic maple syrup:
- ¼ cup balsamic vinegar
- ¼ cup maple syrup

Instructions:

1. First, make the strawberry salsa by combining the salsa ingredients in a small mixing bowl and stirring to combine. Set the bowl to one side.

2. Next, prepare the pancake batter. In a medium bowl, mix all of the dry ingredients.

3. In a blender, blend the milk along with the banana, olive oil, and vanilla until silky smooth. Add this mixture to the dry mixture, together with the egg, stir well to incorporate.

4. In a large, heavy-bottomed pan over moderate heat melt the butter, along with the coconut oil.

5. As soon as the pan is hot, spoon in the batter; ½ cupfuls at a time.

6. After 3-4 minutes, flip, and cook the other side of the pancakes for approximately 3 minutes.

7. While you are cooking the pancakes, make the balsamic maple syrup.

8. In a small sized pan, add the vinegar along with the maple syrup and heat over moderate heat. Occasionally whisk, while cooking for 4-5 minutes, until the mixture has slightly reduced and thickened.

9. To serve. Stack 3 to 4 pancakes, and top with salsa. Drizzle with balsamic maple syrup and serve.

(26) Blueberry Avocado and Chia Breakfast Pudding

This breakfast pudding is packed full of natural ingredients and ensures that you get a great start to your day.

Serving Size: 2

Preparation Time: 50mins

Ingredient List:

- 1 very ripe avocado (peeled, pitted)
- 1 cup fresh or frozen blueberries
- 2 tablespoons coconut milk
- 2 tablespoons maple syrup
- ½ teaspoons vanilla extract
- 1 teaspoon ground chia seeds

||||||||||||||||||||||||||||||||||||||||||||||||||||||||||||||||||||||||

Instructions:

1. Combine all 6 ingredients in a blender and process until silky smooth. Stop the blender every 20 seconds or so, and using a spoon, mix to combine.

2. Evenly divide the mixture between ramekins and transfer to the refrigerator for 30-45 minutes before serving. This will enable the chia to thicken.

(27) Pears Baked in Maple Syrup

Baked pears are a welcome change from the usual pancake or waffle breakfast and are particularly tasty served with porridge or yogurt.

Serving Size: 5

Preparation Time: 23mins

Ingredient List:

- 5 ripe conference pears (peeled, cored, cut in half lengthwise)
- Beans from 1 vanilla pod
- Maple syrup
- Handful hazelnuts (coarsely chopped)

||||||||||||||||||||||||||||||||||||||||||||||||||||||||||||||||||||

Instructions:

1. Preheat the main oven 375 degrees f.

2. Arrange the pear halves on a baking sheet lined with parchment paper.

3. In a small bowl combine the vanilla beans and mix with maple syrup

4. Scatter chopped nuts over the top. Bake 15 minutes.

5. Enjoy with porridge, cream or yogurt.

(28) Breakfast Bacon and Maple Meatballs

A yummy weekend breakfast or brunch dish to share with the family. Serve with over easy eggs.

Serving Size: 4

Preparation Time: 50mins

Ingredient List:

- 5-6 rashers bacon
- 1 medium sweet potato (peeled, chopped)
- ½ yellow onion (peeled)
- 4 ounces button mushrooms (sliced)
- 1 pound breakfast sausage (casings removed)
- 2 tablespoons maple syrup
- 1 clove garlic (minced)
- Sea salt and black pepper

||||||||||||||||||||||||||||||||||||||||||||||||||||||||||||||||||||

Instructions:

1. Preheat the main oven to 375 degrees f.

2. Arrange the rashers of bacon to a frying pan over moderate heat cook until crispy. Pat dry with kitchen paper and chop. Set to one side.

3. Finely shred the sweet potato using a food processor. Add the onion and mushrooms to the processor, still containing the potato, and shred again.

4. Add the shredded vegetables to a mixing bowl along with the sausage, maple syrup, minced garlic, diced bacon, sea salt and black pepper and using clean hands mix to combine well.

5. Line a baking sheet with parchment paper.

6. To make the meatballs. Scoop up the meatball mixture using an ice cream scoop; this will help to make sure they are evenly sized. Roll the scooped out meatballs in your hands and arrange them on the lined baking sheet. Repeat the process until all of the ingredients have been used.

7. Bake in the oven for just over half an hour, or until the meatballs are golden brown and cooked through.

(29) Maple Syrup Blueberry Muffins

Enjoy a blueberry muffin with a hot cup of coffee to go, and those hunger pains are sure to be kept at bay.

Serving Size: 12

Preparation Time: 30mins

Ingredient List:

- 1¾ cup all-purpose flour
- 1½ teaspoons baking powder
- ¼ teaspoons baking soda
- ¼ teaspoons salt
- 1 medium egg (beaten)
- ⅔ cup maple syrup
- ½ cup whole milk
- 6 tablespoons butter (melted)
- 1 cup blueberries

|||||||||||||||||||||||||||||||||||||||||||||||||||||||||||||||||||

Instructions:

1. Preheat the main oven to 400 degrees f. Lightly grease a 12 cup muffin tray.

2. In a medium-sized mixing bowl, whisk the flour together with the baking powder, baking soda, and salt.

3. In small mixing bowl, whisk the egg with the maple syrup, milk, and melted butter. Add this mixture to the flour mixture and stir well until combined.

4. Next, fold in the blueberries

5. Divide the mixture between the 12 muffin cups and bake in the oven for between 15-18 minutes.

(30) Breakfast Lasagne

Instead of pasta this lasagne layers pancakes with eggs, sausage, and a sweet maple syrup béchamel.

Serving Size: 10-12

Preparation Time: 35mins

Ingredient List:

- ¾ pound breakfast sausage (cooked, drained)
- Maple béchamel:
- 3 tablespoons butter
- 2 tablespoons all-purpose flour
- 2 cups whole milk
- ½ cup maple syrup
- ¼ teaspoons salt
- ¼ teaspoons freshly grated nutmeg

Pancakes:

- 3 cups all-purpose flour
- 2 tablespoons + 1 teaspoon baking powder
- 2 teaspoons salt
- 2 tablespoons white sugar
- 2½ cups whole milk
- 2 medium eggs
- 6 tablespoons butter (melted)
- 12 medium eggs (scrambled)
- 1 cup cheddar cheese (finely shredded)

||||||||||||||||||||||||||||||||||||||||||||||||||||||||||||||||||||

Instructions:

1. Cook the sausage and set to one aside.

2. Prepare the béchamel sauce by melting the butter over a moderate heat in a small-sized sauce pan. Once the butter has melted, add the flour and cook until it is a pale gold color, around 4-5 minutes.

3. In the meantime, heat the milk along with the maple syrup until the mixture is hot. As soon as the flavor and butter are ready, add the milk mixture and whisk until silky smooth.

4. Bring the mixture to a boil and reduce the heat down to low, and cook for 8-10 minute, stirring until the mixture thickens. Remove the pan from the heat and season well with salt and nutmeg. Put the pan to one side until needed.

5. Preheat the main oven to 375 degrees f.

6. To make the pancakes. Sift the flour together with the baking powder, salt and sugar into a large bowl. Add the milk, along with the 2 eggs and melted butter; mix until silky smooth.

7. Over a moderate to high heat, heat a lightly oiled frying pan or skillet heat and scoop the batter into the frying pan, using around 1/4 cup for each pancake. Brown the pancake on both sides and put to one side until you are ready to assemble the breakfast lasagne.

8. Prepare and scramble the 12 eggs. In a 9x13" baking pan add ¾ cup of béchamel to the bottom of the baking pan. Next, layer the pancakes. It may make it easier to fit the baking pan by cutting the pancakes into squares.

9. Add the scrambled eggs and cooked sausage and pour 1 cup of béchamel over the sausage. Add another layer of pancake to the cooked sausage, pour 1 cup over béchamel over the top. Top with 1 cup of shredded cheese and the remaining béchamel.

10. Cover the pan with aluminum foil and bake for 15-20 minutes, until the cheese has melted.

11. Serve at once.

(31) Maple Sage Breakfast Patties

You can make these patties with pork or beef but regardless of which meat you choose they are brilliant served with eggs and pancakes.

Serving Size: 8

Preparation Time: 25mins

Ingredient List:

- 2 pounds 100% ground pork
- 3 tablespoons grade b maple syrup
- 3 tablespoons fresh sage (minced)
- ¾ teaspoons sea salt
- ½ teaspoons garlic powder
- 1 teaspoon solid cooking fat

Instructions:

1. Add the pork to a mixing bowl and using the back of a wooden spoon break the meat apart.

2. Drizzle the pork with maple syrup and sprinkle with minced sage, salt, and garlic powder.

3. Using clean hands, mix until combined. Mold the mixture into 8 evenly sized patties and put to one side.

4. In a frying pan or skillet, heat the cooking fat over moderate heat. As soon as the fat melts and the pan is hot, add the pork patties, and cook for 8-10 minutes each side, or until cooked through.

5. Serve with eggs and pancakes.

(32) Carrot Cake Pancakes with Brown Butter Maple Syrup

Totally indulgent and sweet maple syrup butter served with carrot and pumpkin spiced pancakes are the best!

Serving Size: 4

Preparation Time: 35mins

Ingredient List:

- 3 tablespoons butter
- ½ cup maple syrup
- 1¼ cups flour
- 2 teaspoons baking powder
- 1 teaspoon ground cinnamon
- ¼ teaspoons salt
- 1 teaspoon pumpkin pie spice
- ¼ cup brown sugar
- ¾ cup low-fat buttermilk
- 1 tablespoon coconut oil (melted)
- 1½ teaspoons vanilla extract
- 2 medium eggs (lightly beaten)
- 2 cups carrots (finely grated)
- Nonstick cooking spray

Instructions:

1. In a saucepan over moderate heat, melt and brown the 3 tablespoons of butter, occasionally whisking until brown specks begin to appear, and the mixture smells a little nutty. Once the butter is gently browned, add and stir in the maple syrup. Put to one side.

2. In a large mixing bowl whisk in the flour along with the baking powder, cinnamon, salt and pumpkin spice.

3. In a second bowl, combine the brown sugar with the buttermilk, coconut oil, and vanilla extract.

4. Gradually, stir the combined wet ingredients, along with the beaten egg, into the dry ingredients until incorporated. Add the carrots and stir to combine.

5. Over moderate heat, heat a large frying pan or skillet. Lightly coat the pan with nonstick cooking spray.

6. Pour the batter into the pan, ¼ cup at a time and cook for a few minutes, until bubbles begin to form on the top. Flip over and continue cooking for 2-3 minutes.

7. Slowly stir wet ingredients into the dry ingredients until combined. Stir in shredded carrots.

8. Heat a large skillet or griddle over medium heat. Coat with non-stick cooking spray, and pour batter onto the skillet 1/4 cup at a time. Cook for 2-3 minutes or until bubbles appear on the tops. Flip and cook for another 2 minutes.

9. Serve the pancakes warm with brown butter maple syrup.

(33) Maple French Toast Overnight Oatmeal

Prepare this oatmeal on Sunday night, and as Monday morning dawns you will have a healthy and filling start to the week ahead.

Serving Size: 2

Preparation Time: 8hours 5mins

Ingredient List:

- ½ ripe banana (peeled, mashed)
- 1 cup rolled oats
- ½ teaspoons cinnamon
- ½ teaspoons vanilla extract
- 1 tablespoon pure maple syrup
- 1 teaspoon flaxseed meal
- ¾ cup unsweetened milk

Optional toppings:

- Toasted coconut
- Whipped cream
- Banana
- Cinnamon

||||||||||||||||||||||||||||||||||||||||||||||||||||||||||||||||||||||||||

Instructions:

1. In a medium-sized bowl, add the mashed banana to the oats, cinnamon, vanilla extract, maple syrup, flaxseed meal and milk. Stir well to combine and allow to soak overnight.

2. Serve with toasted coconut, whipped cream, banana slices and dust with cinnamon.

(34) Cottage Cheese and Maple Yogurt Parfait

If you store this parfait in a mason jar, you can seal it up and eat it on the go.

Serving Size: 4

Preparation Time: 7mins

Ingredient List:

- 1 cup fresh fruit of choice*
- 1 tablespoon maple syrup
- 2 cups cottage cheese
- 1 cup vanilla yogurt
- 1 cup granola

||||||||||||||||||||||||||||||||||||||||||||||||||||||||||||||||||

Instructions:

1. In a bowl, toss the fruit with the maple syrup to evenly coat. Set to one side.

2. In a second bowl combine the cottage cheese with the yogurt and stir to incorporate.

3. Divide the mixture between 4 mason jars (with lids)

4. Top with the fruit mixture (including any juice from the fruit) and sprinkle with granola.

5. Serve immediately or seal up and go.

* strawberries, bananas, and berries work really well.

(35) Maple Brown Rice Breakfast

Treat yourself to a bowl of maple brown rice, and you will be able to cope with anything the day throws at you.

Serving Size: 2

Preparation Time: 15mins

Ingredient List:

- 2 + cups water
- 1 cup brown dry brown rice
- 1 cup plain coconut milk
- ½ cup unsweetened coconut chips
- ½ cup maple syrup
- ¼ cup sliced almonds
- ¼ cup golden raisins
- Pinch cinnamon
- Pinch salt

Toppings (optional):

- Coconut chips
- Sliced almonds
- Maple syrup
- Splash coconut milk

||||||||||||||||||||||||||||||||||||||||||||||||||||||||||||||||||

Instructions:

1. First, take a pan of water and cook the brown rice according to the package instructions. Drain.

2. As soon as the rice is cooked, add the coconut milk, coconut chips, maple syrup, sliced almonds, golden raisins, a pinch of cinnamon and salt.

3. Cook while stirring over a moderate to low heat until the milk starts to absorb and the mixture begins to thicken, around 5-10 minutes.

4. Top with coconut chips, sliced almonds, and drizzle with maple syrup and a dash of milk.

5. Enjoy warm or cold.

(36) Fruit Omelet with Maple Syrup Yogurt

You can use either canned or fresh fruit in this scrummy omelet.

Serving Size: 4

Preparation Time: 10mins

Ingredient List:

- 7 large eggs
- 1 cup fruit yogurt (flavor of choice)
- ¼ cup maple syrup
- ½ cup 15% cream
- 2 tablespoons butter
- 6 fresh strawberries (hulled)
- 6 slices of ripe banana
- 8 seedless green grapes
- Maple syrup

IIIIIIIIIIIIIIIIIIIIIIIIIIIIIIIIIIIIIIIIIIIIIIIIIIIIIIIIIIIIIIIIIIIIII

Instructions:

1. In a mixing bowl, whisk the eggs for 25-30 seconds.

2. Add the yogurt, maple syrup, and cream, stirring, until the mixture is silky smooth. Set to one side.

3. In a large frying pan or skillet, melt the butter over a moderate heat and add the egg mixture.

4. Cover the pan and cook the omelet for 6-8 minutes, or until you achieve your preferred level of doneness.

5. Top the omelet with lots of fresh fruit and drizzle with maple syrup, continue cooking for 2 minutes.

6. Remove from the heat and serve.

(37) Maple Berry Breakfast Clafoutis

Clafoutis is a fruity baked french dessert, put together in a buttered dish and covered with a flan-like thick batter. This version used blackberries rather than the traditional black cherries.

Serving Size: 8

Preparation Time: 8hours 55mins

Ingredient List:

- Coconut oil (to grease)
- 3 cups blackberries (washed, patted dry)
- 4 medium eggs
- ⅓ cup grade b pure maple syrup
- 1 cup whole milk
- Zest 1 lemon
- 1 teaspoon vanilla extract
- ½ teaspoons salt
- ½ cup gluten-free flour
- ½ teaspoons cinnamon

||||||||||||||||||||||||||||||||||||||||||||||||||||||||||||||||||||

Instructions:

1. Preheat the main oven to 350 degrees f. Lightly grease a skillet with coconut oil.

2. Scatter the blackberries into the skillet.

3. In a bowl, whisk together the eggs along with the maple syrup, whole milk, lemon zest, vanilla, and salt, mixing until incorporated.

4. Gradually add the flour and cinnamon and whiskey until lump free.

5. Carefully pour the batter over the blackberries and bake in the oven for 30 minutes, until the pie is puffy, golden brown and just set.

6. Allow to cool, before transferring to the fridge overnight.

7. Slice and serve either warm or chilled.

(38) Greek Yogurt Breakfast Bark

Pop this snack into your snack box and enjoy this breakfast-on-the-go bark.

Serving Size: 6

Preparation Time: 8hours 10mins

Ingredient List:

- 1½ cups plain greek yogurt
- 3 tablespoons maple syrup
- ½ cup blueberry pecan granola
- 4 fresh strawberries (washed, hulled, sliced)
- ½ cup blueberries

‖‖‖

Instructions:

1. Line a baking tray with parchment paper and put to one side.

2. In a medium mixing bowl, combine the yogurt along with the syrup and stir until incorporated. Pour the mixture onto the baking sheet, and evenly spread in a thin layer.

3. Top with the granola, sliced strawberries, and blueberries. Cover the tray with aluminum foil and transfer to the freezer overnight.

4. Break the bark into pieces and enjoy.

(39) Maple Bacon Breakfast Pie

This dish combines the best breakfast ingredients in one gorgeous pie.

Serving Size: 8

Preparation Time: 1hour 15mins

Ingredient List:

- 4 large eggs
- 2 cups whole milk
- ¾ teaspoons sea salt
- ¼ teaspoons freshly ground black pepper
- 1 cup cheddar cheese (shredded)
- 2 cups potatoes (diced)
- 3 green onions (sliced)
- 3 slices thick cut bacon (cooked, crumbled)
- 1 (9") refrigerated pie crust
- 10-12 rashers thick cut bacon
- Maple syrup (for brushing)

||||||||||||||||||||||||||||||||||||||||||||||||||||||||||||||||||||

Instructions:

1. Preheat the main oven to 350 degrees f.

2. In a mixing bowl, whisk the eggs along with the whole milk, sea salt, and freshly ground black pepper.

3. Add the shredded cheese, diced potatoes, onions and crumbled bacon and stir well to incorporate.

4. Put the pie crust in the base of a 9" pie dish.

5. Pour the egg mixture into the pie crust. Place in the oven and bake for just over 35 minutes or until the pie is sufficiently firm enough to lay the bacon on.

6. Remove the pie from the oven and turn the oven temperature up to 450 degrees f.

7. Carefully weave bacon rashers into a lattice design on top of the quiche. Brush the bacon slices with maple syrup.

8. Cover the edges of the pie with foil as this will prevent the crust from burning.

9. Return the pie to the oven and bake for a further 12-15 minutes.

10. Remove the pie from the oven.

11. Over the kitchen sink, carefully tip the pie to drain off any excess bacon fat.

12. Allow the pie to rest for 4-5 minutes and serve.

(40) Lemon Cream Cheese Pancakes with Blueberry Maple Syrup

Tart lemon combines with sweet maple syrup to whip up a batch of pancakes.

Serving Size: 2-4

Preparation Time: 25mins

Ingredient List:

- 1 batch fresh pancakes (from homemade pancake mix)
- 4 tablespoons cream cheese (softened)
- 1 teaspoon freshly grated lemon zest
- Pat butter
- 1½ cups fresh blueberries
- 1 cup maple syrup

||||||||||||||||||||||||||||||||||||||||||||||||||||||||||||||||||||||||

Instructions:

1. Whip up one batch of pancakes using the pancake mix and whisk in the cream cheese to the pancake mix until it's in small pieces. Stir in the lemon zest.

2. In a frying pan or skillet over moderate heat, melt a pat of butter and cook the pancakes until golden brown on each side.

3. Make the sauce by adding the blueberries and the maple syrup to a small-sized saucepan and warm over a moderate heat. Gently warm the berries, swirling the saucepan, until the berries begin to soften and burst. This will take around 10 minutes.

4. Stack the pancakes and pour the blueberry sauce over the top.

About the Author

Nancy Silverman is an accomplished chef from Essex, Vermont. Armed with her degree in Nutrition and Food Sciences from the University of Vermont, Nancy has excelled at creating e-books that contain healthy and delicious meals that anyone can make and everyone can enjoy. She improved her cooking skills at the New England Culinary Institute in Montpelier Vermont and she has been working at perfecting her culinary style since graduation. She claims that her life's work is always a work in progress and she only hopes to be an inspiration to aspiring chefs everywhere.

Her greatest joy is cooking in her modern kitchen with her family and creating inspiring and delicious meals. She often says that she has perfected her signature dishes based on her family's critique of each and every one.

Nancy has her own catering company and has also been fortunate enough to be head chef at some of Vermont's most exclusive restaurants. When a friend suggested she share some of her outstanding signature dishes, she decided to add cookbook author to her repertoire of personal achievements. Being a technological savvy woman, she felt the e-book realm would be a better fit and soon she had her first cookbook available online. As of today, Nancy has sold over 1,000 e-books and has shared her culinary experiences and brilliant recipes with people from all over the world! She plans on expanding into self-help books and dietary cookbooks, so stayed tuned!

Author's Afterthoughts

Thank you for making the decision to invest in one of my cookbooks! I cherish all my readers and hope you find joy in preparing these meals as I have.

There are so many books available and I am truly grateful that you decided to buy this one and follow it from beginning to end.

I love hearing from my readers on what they thought of this book and any value they received from reading it. As a personal favor, I would appreciate any feedback you can give in the form of a review on Amazon and please be honest! This kind of support will help others make an informed choice on and will help me tremendously in producing the best quality books possible.

My most heartfelt thanks,

Nancy Silverman

If you're interested in more of my books, be sure to follow my author page on Amazon (can be found on the link Bellow) or scan the QR-Code.

https://www.amazon.com/author/nancy-silverman

Made in the USA
Las Vegas, NV
06 November 2023

80344564R00069